T0068258

NEVER LET THE TEARS, STOP YOU FROM LAUGHING

D. Richard Truman

NEVER LET THE TEARS,
STOP YOU FROM LAUGHING

iUniverse books may be ordered through booksellers or by contacting:

iUniverse
1663 Liberty Drive
Bloomington, IN 47403
www.iuniverse.com
844-349-9409

ISBN: 978-1-6632-5534-1 (sc)
ISBN: 978-1-6632-5535-8 (e)

Library of Congress Control Number: 2023915216

Print information available on the last page.

iUniverse rev. date: 09/13/2023

COMMENTS

Thanks to the many I've encountered on this long journey through life, who have shared laughter and cracking up with me when, I needed it most.

To those who touched my life most and will never be forgotten: Charles and Doreen Holland, Wilbert and Emma Annabelle Truman, my late brothers Robert/Bob and Harry Truman, and David Hutchinson. To my family that helps keep me on the straight and narrow: Joyce and Ross Hurd and family, Marion, Christopher, and Drew Hutchinson, Sylvia, David, Maureen, and Joseph Truman. To my children and grandchildren, Michelle, Adam, Alex, Ryan and Kylie Stafford and Nicole Truman, Oliver and Sebastian Hall. To my wife Beverley, who has the patience of a saint for listening to all of my ideas while travelling through life, I thank you.

You've lived life to the full,
now let's leave the cloistered towers
of goodwill, until the end of time.

CONTENTS

CHAPTER 1
First there was light.

When light reached into my crib, I reached back and assured everyone that life had begun. With my first awareness of light, my eyes began to water, and much later, I picked up a pencil and felt another passion: to scribble something different and uniquely mine, because that was what I wanted to do. It was a time before the hurried rush into the future, before being immersed in a mad and crazy world of computers, the internet, touchscreens, passwords, laptops, tablets, and absolute nonsense that I would spend years chasing to catch up.

But first, let's step way back a couple of hundred years to say thank you to the French for the birth of the pencil, which the French call "le crayon." Yes, the silly but practical pencil first appeared way back in 1795, well before I was conceived.

A brutal-looking scientist in Napoleon Bonaparte's army, by the name of Nicholas-Jacques Conte, toyed with graphite sticks wrapped in a bit of wood, which allowed anyone to scribble anything they wished on what was called paper or "papier" in French, or whatever. If you didn't like what you scribbled, you could actually rub it out and do it again. Presto! It was a breakthrough compared to the burdensome quill pen, which wouldn't let you erase anything after you scribbled on parchment. Frustration for sure, but the graphite stick wrapped in wood allowed you to rub the image out and do it again correctly, with no frustration. Rub, rub, rub, and it's gone, allowing you to draw or print a word the way you wanted it to be done. In my life, it was pure magic.

Yes, the world of creativity made a giant breakthrough when the world welcomed the loving pencil or "le crayon" to create magic words or drawings.

Maybe that is where it all began, after I scrambled from the crib and opened my eyes to be met with so many loving faces. Yes, I soon discovered the pencil, which also led me to a career that would take a few years to develop, with color and complex drawings - but more about that in the next few chapters.

It wasn't long after being a child that I realized I was a person, and I began to make decisions for myself, like pointing, listening, and making choices. I soon realized I had a degree of power over my hands, arms, whole body, and mind, and I could talk back, make decisions, and take actions that were my own. I could even decide whether I liked peanut butter or marmalade and eat directly from a jar or spread something on bread. By the age of five, I was a real person, and I told Mum and Dad what I wanted to be, something different - in the early days, it was called an originator or a creative guy. Yes, I was going to be alright. Then I discovered the mirror and could look at myself, *telling myself* that I was going to be something big one day due to my creative flair and unique nature. I wouldn't mind if they laughed at me. One day, I learned that it meant "involving the imagination or developing original ideas in the production of artistic work." So, I thanked my tiny dictionary for the clarity it provided. It was a start.

CHAPTER 2
Next. There are words.

As I entered kindergarten, the vast world opened its doors to me, and "words" took on meaning. Words became my new avenue for thinking as I delved into a 4 page big book, learning to read those big words.

Reading became my passion, especially after my wonderful teacher, Miss Humphrey, told me a story I will always remember.

She said, "My language is English, a soup of words that evolved during the Anglo-Saxon times, borrowing from Old English, Norman, Northern German, Danish, and Norwegian. These languages were fused together over six centuries, from 410 to 1066. At first, everyone simply communicated through grunts and squeaks, taking nearly 956 years to develop them into a more understandable form. They didn't include any dirty words, however. Eventually, scholars put a stop to this chaos and compiled what was called a dictionary, which contained 180,976 words in the newfound English language." The scholars were overjoyed, exclaiming, "This is madness! Soon we'll have to look at going back to the caves again."

I was thrilled at the prospect of arranging these words and doodling pictures with a pencil to communicate interesting thoughts. And that was just English; I could also learn French and many other languages. However, there were almost 7,000 additional languages in the world, with English as the leader. I thought my head would explode with creative thoughts to support my scribbles.

By the time I reached the ripe age of ten, my thoughts were still jumbled, but I didn't mind as I enjoyed thinking differently from my friends. I dressed oddly, perhaps because my mum and dad couldn't afford proper clothes, and I had to make do with hand-me-downs from others or from what was known as the Amity. Despite that, I felt loved and protected, knowing that my big brother and parents were there to support me, even ready to throw a punch if someone got in my way. My mum was fierce; she'd squeeze the nose of any bully and give them a whack around the ears with her glaring eyes. Then she'd comfort me by giving me a popsicle, the remedy for all kids' trials and tribulations. Life continued harmoniously with our neighbors, thanks to the kiddy-love sermons from Christ delivered by the church minister.

Being young also had its challenges—girls. During the ogling phase, we'd exchange glances, giggle, and smile, leaving me feeling both embarrassed and intrigued. They taught me about love, though I couldn't quite grasp its meaning. By the age of twelve, I was already experiencing the changes of growing up, with holes in my socks, tighter pants, and maybe the hint of a mustache or remnants of a chocolate bar.

One skill I never lost, however, was the ability to pick up a pencil and draw. I would sketch everything, including my first love—my blonde fluffy-haired sweetheart. It was a decent drawing, and I kept it for years as a memento of growing up and the idea of getting married to my first love. It was also the beginning of my secret album, where I stored personal memories that no one else was allowed to see. My little angel with fluffy blonde hair remained in my heart, and our love story endured for many years.

The magic pencil became my prized possession,

serving as my first camera, capturing images of everything I loved. The results still reside in my secret archive of early memories, cherished until I began accumulating real-life experiences to remember. At school, a bully shouted at me to "grow up," but I decided not to conform; I liked who I was and wanted to think and be myself, not one of the robotic kids at school. When a fat kid called me "Hey kid, you've got a screw loose!" I punched him on the nose, and for months, I was hailed as a hero on the block. I had indeed grown up, in my own unique way.

CHAPTER 3
Dreaming of what I want to be: or should I simply stop dreaming and just do it?

When do we ever know what we want to be, and how the heck do we get there? In all honesty, we never truly know because the possibilities are endless. We could be an astronaut, a doctor, a politician, a physics teacher, a taxi driver, or even a quirky and inventive writer.

But who should have the most influence on us? Is it our friends, parents, grandparents, books, television, heroes, or the movies? No, it's usually something unexpected, like a feeling, a dream, or perhaps the desire to be rich or famous. For me, it was a dedicated teacher who recognized my potential in grade eight and said, "...you appear to be interested and good at..." By grade nine, I was on a mission. My trusty pencil and the dictionary under my arm had uncovered a deeply hidden aspiration— to become a creative force and find financial success that would allow me to lead a comfortable life. Then, I could find someone as wonderful as my first love, and together, we would embark on a career that would bring happiness and joy to everyone around us. Having a family with too would be a dream come true. Above all, I was determined to be what I wanted to be, and I knew I could make it happen. Of course, every step in life comes with its share of challenges and obstacles, but I was prepared to take the necessary risks, and I would do it with a smile.

CHAPTER 4
Nothing will get in the way!

T he most important thing to remember is that there are things out there that might get in the way. But you have to spot them early and work through, over, or around them. Number 1, though, is your desire to win while enjoying the rocky ride. You have to spot the obstacles early and work damn hard to focus on them and work like a hungry savage to get around or, yes, even over them.

First, there is the need for something called money, which you'll need to attend an accredited educational facility. Yes, that takes money, and no one will help you. You have to work for a while and save the necessary money. Don't expect someone to pay the way; it is up to you. You may get lucky and find someone or an opportunity that can help, but that's a backup. Never give up; it could take years to reach a level of excellence to advance your career, just keep going.

Second, the competition in the market; fellow job seekers and employees can create hell for you and trip you up to prevent you from achieving greater goals. Unless, of course, you are showing a very unique set of skills. Be careful how and where you tread, and always do it with a dash of humor and an abundance of likability. It is amazing how this attribute will be seen and seized upon, and suddenly you'll have a career for life with endless possibilities. Watch the legal steps too, that you might be about to take with great care as well; you can be blindsided by greedy corporations ready to deal you out because of one little misstep for some silly and selfish reason, like a desperate corporate merger or a business maneuver that will benefit the chief honcho.

Success may seem simple, but it is not, providing you are aware of the efforts you must make and the unique talents you possess, so keep laughing; and watch yourself be on your way.

CHAPTER 5
When you smell success, grip it tightly.

B efore I knew it, I had graduated, thanks to my attentive teacher who recognized my strengths and guided me in the right direction.

At seventeen, I found myself working part-time, stocking shelves in a food store. It was my very first job, and little did I know that it was the beginning of a journey that would last until my retirement when I would proudly hang up my hat, declaring, "That was an exciting, fun-filled adventure!"

The right path for me led me to the wonderful world of advertising, where I could work with words and pictures to create advertising ideas that sold products. It was a straightforward concept: if my ideas didn't sell products, I would be out the door and never find myself in that profession again. A reality that kept me motivated.

My love for words, all 180,976 of them, and my continued passion for the modern version of the pencil drove me to create compelling images and select just the right words to sell and communicate ideas effectively. Nothing could deter me. In fact, I consider myself lucky to have stumbled upon a remarkable opportunity during the swinging and singing Sixties by landing a job in London, England – the epicenter of cultural and inventive revolution of the century. It was a decade like no other in history.

Suddenly, and perhaps serendipitously, I found myself recording soundtracks for TV, film, and radio campaigns alongside some of the world's top recording artists. Soon enough, they became my dear friends and allies in this exciting journey.

CHAPTER 6
All of a sudden, the jump was pretty obvious.

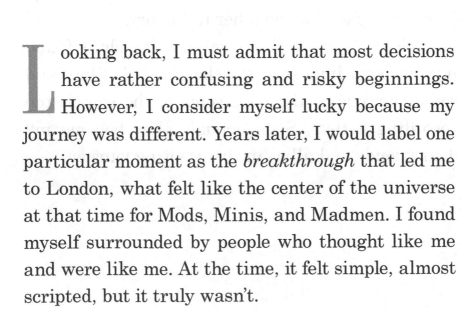

L ooking back, I must admit that most decisions have rather confusing and risky beginnings. However, I consider myself lucky because my journey was different. Years later, I would label one particular moment as the *breakthrough* that led me to London, what felt like the center of the universe at that time for Mods, Minis, and Madmen. I found myself surrounded by people who thought like me and were like me. At the time, it felt simple, almost scripted, but it truly wasn't.

My ascent began gradually as I achieved success while working as a Creative Director at a top advertising agency called MacLarens in Toronto. I was tasked with writing television commercials for General Motors, specifically the bulk of Chevrolet's business in Canada.

One project I worked on was the launch of a new hatchback car called the Chevy Vega. With my trusty pencil, I started writing a script and sketching storyboard frames to convey the look, words, and pace of the upcoming TV commercial. After enduring a grinding process of meetings, technical approvals, and competitive estimates, we selected the talented director, Scott Hamilton, to bring the commercial to life on film. Eventually, the commercial made its debut on air, just like any other big-budget television launch, complete with hoopla, excitement, and a bit of agony. However, it appeared to have that elusive quality they call "magic."

Soon, I moved on to launch another car on television, and the ritualistic process began anew. Though nothing was easy, the creative teams found it entirely fun, except for the "fat cat" decision-makers at General Motors who faced the agony of making choices.

When the agency sensed that a commercial was good, we eagerly entered it into TV award shows across North America and around the world. Winning awards at these shows was a source of pride for the agency and the General Motors marketing team.

The celebration parties that followed were quite the reason to cheer, not to mention the positive impact on paychecks. Winning awards ensured smiles all around and reassured the agency that they were unlikely to lose this valuable business anytime soon.

Then, unexpectedly, something extraordinary happened after we entered the Hollywood Radio and TV awards. The agency won a gold medal for the Vega TV launch commercial. There were cheers and congratulations, with the usual half a dozen people taking credit for the creative effort, but ultimately, my name was on the award. I was the magic man who casually made it happen, and that meant a great deal more to me.

Meanwhile, significant events were taking place worldwide around the same time, events that would soon shine a massive spotlight in my direction.

CHAPTER 7

I can hear it, I can see it, and I like it.

A s the competition sensed an opportunity, doors began to swing open, and good fortune fell into place, starting across the Atlantic with Chrysler UK. The large but struggling automaker was undergoing a reorganization, and in an effort to rescue the sinking company, they appointed a Canadian, Don Lander, as Chairman, and another Canadian as the head of marketing to lead its marketing department in England. They believed that North Americans had the audacity to successfully market cars and turn a profit. So, the Canadians at Chrysler devised a plan.

Meanwhile, an agency called Grant Worldwide

had plans to acquire a British advertising agency in London. Suddenly, several agencies from around the world were vying for the Chrysler UK business, and Grant saw an opportunity.

Enter Joe "Big Boots," a clever individual heading up Grant's Toronto and worldwide offices. He was encouraged to get involved in an aggressive pitch to win the Chrysler business, which seemed like an immense and almost unbelievable challenge, contingent on numerous factors. However, the Canadian connections were the key.

Meanwhile, Joe "Big Boots" had been closely following the Hollywood marketing awards and had taken note of a talented individual in Toronto who had just won a major award at the Hollywood Radio and TV awards for their work with General Motors. This person was none other than the aforementioned "kid" from Toronto, who had demonstrated remarkable creative prowess.

Big Boots saw an opportunity and thought to himself, "Why not hire this kid to lead a Canadian-staffed team for Chrysler UK? With a group of skilled Canadians already in place, he could send this talented individual to London on a 5-year contract to take charge of the Chrysler UK creative business at Grant Advertising, the recently acquired agency." It would be a convergence of new and aggressive Canadian minds, now stationed in the UK with Canadian experience on standby. The risk was significant, but if it worked, it would be a colossal success, bringing recognition to many notable individuals involved.

CHAPTER 8

It started with a ring-ring from Joe saying "Richard - let's make a deal"?

O ut of the blue, Joe "Big Boots" called at the end of another long day and said, "Hello Richard, I'm Joe from blah blah blah! Let's talk.

I want to talk turkey," he barked. "I can arrange a five-year contract for you in London, working for Chrysler UK in our office—transfer, of course. We'll even ship your girlfriend's horse to London if you wish."

Somehow, he knew my future wife had a horse. The rest is history, but it took years before I realized this was the biggest breakthrough in my early career.

Events fell into place. I was struck by an earth-shattering event, all because of competing global automobile giants, Chrysler and General Motors. A few multi-million dollar purchases and a Hollywood award, and I might have landed the job of a lifetime in the "Swingin' London" revolution that was exploding, making London the center of the universe for practically everything creative and innovative. I also discovered that I was joining a bevy of 60,000 new Canadians attracted to the global revolution in London, all set to land in the UK that year.

Opportunity strikes at the oddest of times in the oddest of ways. When it does, grab it, take the risk, and never let go!

A couple of weeks later, after selling my house in Toronto, I settled in the beautiful country town of Guildford, England. It was time to meet the staff and fellow workers at Grant Advertising in Knightsbridge, just a short walk to the hippest street in London and the world: King's Road. It was beautiful craziness, exploding in all directions.

The first morning at Grant Advertising was dedicated to finding staff—art directors, writers, and producers—to prepare for this potential addition of business with the multimillion-pound Chrysler advertising account. This was "Big Boots" at his best, always taking big gambles. Now we had to wait, but we felt in our gut that it was really possible. Winning the Chrysler UK account might happen, and if it did, we had hit the big time. First, it had to happen, and Chrysler better have huge plans for growth and success. As for me, if it didn't happen, would I be shipped back to Canada? I looked out from my office window overlooking Sloan and Knightsbridge and felt energized by the colossal but nearly impossible challenge ahead. I was off for a pint with my new friends.

At lightning speed, it was done. "Big Boots" announced we'd actually been awarded the multi-million dollar Chrysler UK account. Now what?

But now I had to build Grant and hire smart staff. Most of the prospects were from the UK regions, and I had to battle little "accent" issues, but they had no problem understanding a Canuck. Next, I had to meet up with Don Lander, the Canadian assigned to Chrysler UK, and his mercurial Canadian team, and I felt right at home. A train ride later after meeting the Chrysler team, I was back in Knightsbridge where the challenges would fall before my new team with wide open minds. Everything was a laugh; it was like a rebirth, everything was new, yet very old for tired minds. Sure, I knew about the Sunbeam and the Avenger cars in the UK, but I knew little about the competitive models by others in the car-crazy

UK. The motto at that time was "never complain – just love the pain."

Before I knew it, I was on the road. The first filming assignment was selling Chrysler's "unsold and used" cars on dealership lots across the land. In a rush of excitement, we hired a familiar actor to Brits—Sid James was chosen as the spokesperson for the television pitch. Sid was the mad South African who was a big television and film funny man

and probably a good choice to excite the British about cars. The Canadians didn't have a clue who he was. I soon learned that Sid was a star in the "Carry On" series that had electrified the nation for years. He was downright hilarious and began the filming day with his bottle of Scotch whisky, which was planted on the lunch table and had all of us rolling around the set by sunset. He was a natural clown and a man endeared by the nation. Yes, he did "fart" for an extra dash of humor. It was a wrap, but it quickly fell on the editor's floor as it was deemed a bit too crass.

Two days later, we were on another set at Pinewood studio doing our first "video shoot," something new for the Brit cinematographers who were used to "filming" with real film. After firing the actor for a lousy performance, it was completed by another actor, and it was time to buddy up at the famous Pinewood bar and hang out with big-name actors.

While snuggling up at Pinewood's bar, I bumped into Roger Moore, the actor loved by the Brits as "The Saint," which was seen by the nation on black and white television. This time Roger was shooting a 007 feature film. After chatting a bit, I asked him a question, "What is your reason for your success and why are you loved by the masses?" His answer was rapid fire when he said it was something he learned from his mother, 'Always listen first, then pause and respond with a short reply that is crystal clear, with no fluffing around, just an intelligent focused response.' We clinked glasses and went back to our film studios at Pinewood. He was an incredible and charming man, and I watched "The Saint," his TV series, for years. But I wasn't quite sure about what his mother had meant.

Then I had another interruption in my now crazy days. Another account appeared before us, and it was purely Canadian. We had just won the Wardair account, an airline that was growing rapidly on the UK-Canada route for leisure travelers. The key man was ex-Canadian bush pilot Max Ward. He was in town showing off his brand new 747s, and his first 747 was about to land at Gatwick. Our first assignment, among many, was to photograph their first brand new 747 landing at Gatwick for advertising purposes. The agency arranged for 3 photographers to be positioned at three locations to capture this historic moment. It was a perfect weather day for a very simple first assignment. Normally, a 747 flies with four engines, but this one had a surprise. Tension was mounting as we awaited the arrival of the plane as it was about to land.

Out of the blue, it appeared on the horizon, but something was odd—my phone began to ring, asking a stupid question, "What are we going to do? This plane has 5 engines?" A crowd of models waiting to have their pictures taken, do interviews, and perform in a video for advertising purposes were in a panic. "Crap!" everyone shouted. "Just take the photos, and we'll airbrush out the fifth engine." Later, we discovered that these mighty aircraft often carry extra engines as a cheap way of delivering spare ones. This one was for the Gatwick maintenance office. The tale circulated for years.

Another story that was circulating was that Max Ward was heard saying he was about to announce to the flying world that he was going to rename the airline "RareAir"—the wonder airline—as he didn't particularly like his name painted on all of his aircraft, and it didn't sound right. But it was denied, of course.

Then I rushed back to the Grant offices with my team to adjust for the next hurried "on-location" shoot in Morocco. The pressure was enormous, as much had to be done to meet media deadlines, with no time wasted.

We had to film a cinema commercial, in Panavision, for Chrysler. It was for the new Alpines positioned as the "economy car" of the year. I was warned it would be a wicked assignment filled with potential problems. The shoot would be managed by a British Director, French crew, and my potential language problems. The script for disaster was soon apparent.

The point of the communication was that the Chrysler Alpine was excellent on mileage, well-engineered, with great durability, no matter the weather. In fact, the message said it could cross the sun-baked Sahara desert with a minimum amount of petrol. Sure, we said!

Finally, we flew to Casablanca, the two cars were shipped to the harbor, then towed over the Atlas Mountains, hidden in a trailer, to a fly-trap town called Zagora. The French film crew and our British Director had not done their homework. When we arrived, it was bloody hot, and according to the local police, there was no lodging available for the first night. After a struggle, we finally got a place to sleep in a police cell. I soon sensed the French do not get along with the Moroccans. They both speak French, but they refuse to understand each other and don't like each other. So I stepped in with my clumsy French and found a solution, sort of. We slept at the police station, in cells for safety, and that was it.

So we tucked into our portable beds to attempt sleeping. We thought! What we hadn't planned on was that we had neighbors in the cells—on the floor. Thousands of bugs were crawling everywhere on the floor and up the walls—yes, the same kind we also call bedbugs. We did our best to crush them and sweep them up, but bedbugs like to play at night as they go looking for food. Yes, it was a terrible night. No one slept, but bug funerals were rampant.

In the morning, we jumped in our backup Alpine and headed to the location to commence production.

We had two brand new Alpines for filming—one for the actual filming, the other was a backup. The night before, we left a shiny new Alpine parked at a location on the edge of the desert, pointed it east to capture the rising sun, and covered it with a shawl to keep the sand and bugs away.

We were ready. The French film crew and I drove the short distance to begin the work of capturing images. But there was a problem. The car we left the night before had disappeared. We saw tire tracks in the sand, along with camel footprints heading out across the desert. They had headed northeast and were gone, and couldn't be found.

The Moroccan police spent a month looking for

our brand-spanking-new Alpine. The car was never found, but the locals were so nice. Oddly, our bellies were full of laughter. Expect the unexpected when you are in unfamiliar settings, speaking an unfamiliar version of a language that no one understands, but this nutcase was all predicted. And they all appeared to have a smile painted on their faces—what the hell do they know that we don't know? Sure, we are all twits. But we'll never film in Morocco again. But I did learn that Morocco is spelled "Maroc" in French. So what, I thought!

So we hopped on a plane in Marrakech and headed over the mountains to Heathrow airport, laughing all the way without the aid of a drink or three. Insurance covered the loss, and we used the backup car to finish filming the commercial. Sorry, Don Lander, no, we didn't tell the big boss the real facts. It's still a mystery to the big guys at Chrysler.

CHAPTER 9
Is it all insanity, in a supposedly disciplined business?

T he most thrilling opportunity for creative individuals is to be part of the development of a brand-new car tailored precisely to meet a specific need in the UK. And the best part is that the budget is limitless; the motto is "spend, spend, spend." However, the challenge is to ensure that the car becomes a massive success because Don of Chrysler UK has staked his reputation on it. The eyes of the bigwigs in Detroit are on him, perhaps waiting to see the outcome with amusement.

Don backed up his words by calling Joe "Big Boots" in Toronto urgently, needing to discuss the matter. Subsequently, Joe contacted my new boss, the remarkable Mr. Brian from London, and demanded his presence, declaring it a high-stakes venture with substantial financial rewards.

I gathered my creative team and Mike's media experts, eagerly awaiting the project brief, considering the multi-million budget. We wondered whether Joe was just bluffing or attempting to scare us.

Unbeknownst to us, the resourceful Joe "Big Boots" had discovered a talented singer, Petula Clark, with a golden voice performing in Las Vegas. He contacted her, urging her to launch the car in England through television or any other means, assuring her that money was no object. Initially, Petula was perplexed, and though it's rumored she said no, the allure of money proved persuasive. Thus, I received a call to assemble my team for this extraordinary project, as everyone was excited to work with Petula Clark, a beloved star since her childhood singing during the war.

The catch was that the new car had no name, no one knew what it looked like, and everyone was navigating the project without a clear direction. Yet, the motivating factor for all involved was the potential financial gain.

My creative team in London, including David and others, gathered over lunch and, true to London tradition, hashed out an idea fueled by a few drinks. Within an hour, they conceived a brilliant plan.

They proposed writing a song for Petula to record and broadcast, along the lines of "Put a little sunshine in your life, it'll put a smile on your face." If it became a hit, they planned to rework the song for commercials, replacing "sunshine" with the name of the new Chrysler car. However, they needed approval from her music publisher CBS for this plan. The team worried that convincing a prominent figure like Petula to agree to this arrangement might be a challenge, but they were determined to make it work.

Eventually, everything fell into place miraculously. Petula agreed to the idea, and with her onboard, they were ready to proceed. They decided to credit her with the song and lyrics and allow her to keep all the royalties from sales, even though it meant foregoing royalties themselves.

Later, Petula acknowledged the collaborative effort, crediting Gus Galbraith for the song and my team for the lyrics in her comprehensive history of the events. This act of generosity made her even more endearing to us.

The creative process began, and I flew to Geneva, where Petula lived, to meet with her. She loved the song idea created by Gus Galbraith, and after a minor adjustment to the lyrics and rhythm, they had a finalized deal. Recording took place at PYE studios in London, an unforgettable event attended by the entire team.

The London creative team crafted compelling television and cinema commercials, which were subsequently approved by CBS, and production began. Richard Lester, a renowned 60s film director who had directed the Beatles' hit film "A Hard Day's Night," was recruited to join the project. His enthusiasm for working with Petula further fueled the excitement.

The entire process was a rollercoaster of madness, excitement, and near-insanity. However, the shared positive energy steered everything in the right direction, uniting us as a fantastic team and leading us to another marketing triumph with Petula, our beloved star.

Petula entering her Sunbeam.

CHAPTER 10
The brightest side of life.

I t took place in Paris, where my star producer, the charming and recently deceased Geoffrey Forster, orchestrated a plan to celebrate the collaboration of Petula Clark, director Richard Lester, and our advertising team, David and myself. We gathered in Paris so that Petula could meet Richard, fostering a comfortable environment to discuss ideas for the upcoming filming and recording of the campaign. To this day, Petula remains our cherished angel, a sentiment shared by anyone who knows her.

A person named Richard treated the agency team to a $7,000 bottle of Armagnac, the "Chateau de Lacquy," to enjoy during a celebratory cruise along the Seine River aboard a luxurious liner. The cruise turned out to be helped by a humorously dubbed version of Robespierre, a name coined by our creative team. It became an unforgettable memory cruise, unlike anything we had experienced before, and I believe it was all planned by the legendary Geoffrey Forster, Britain's finest producer. But let's start from the beginning of the shipboard adventure.

As we walked aboard, we gripped the sturdy railing of the ramp. A stylish assistant, clad in tight-fitting whites with gold braid on her shoulders, took our hands and guided us to safety, leading us to the upper deck for a brief tour. The cruise ship faced Notre Dame, while the grandeur of Eiffel's masterpiece loomed over us from the opposite bank.

Plush seats covered in white leather awaited us on the upper deck. In front of us stood a polished teak table adorned with candles, their flames reflecting on the gleaming surface.

Now, the crew members gazed at us, almost anticipating a speech, or perhaps wondering who we were. One of them seemed oddly disappointed. They were waiting for us to select a drink from the tray offered by Orpine, whose name I found quite charming. We chose wine and settled down, open to the sky, eagerly awaiting Richard Lester and Petula Clark's arrival. This time, I resolved to sit between them to steer the conversation and reach agreements on various matters.

After half an hour, the captain announced the commencement of the cruise, and the crew members swiftly prepared for the journey.

The girls were teasingly attractive and impeccably groomed. A brief whistle was followed by a hushed purr as the cruise ship gracefully departed from the pier. My partner and I exchanged puzzled glances and whispered, "What's going on?" At the four-seat table illuminated by flickering candles, only the two of us sat while the crew bustled about, occasionally casting glances our way.

Various wild thoughts crossed our minds. Were Petula and Richard stood us up, or had we boarded the wrong ship? Was this an elaborate joke, and they never intended to join the cruise in the first place? But soon, we let go of those thoughts and focused on enjoying the evening.

As the overhead lights switched on, we removed our sunglasses. Thousands of tiny golden lights adorned the railings, twinkling in the evening sky. An ensemble of musicians emerged, playing Debussy to commemorate the centenary of his birth. Drinks and hors d'oeuvres flowed, and Champagne was served by the "six-legged bar service": three waiters serving the two of us.

The view was a mesmerizing cathedral of light as we glided past the Pont de L'Alma. The soft music, the sound of rushing water, and the hum of powerful engines set the stage for our intoxicated laughter. The Eiffel Tower waved goodbye as we cruised east, passing by the gardens and the Place du Canada. Just ahead, we approached the magnificent Pont de Invalides, and then we sailed beneath the enchanting Pont Alexandre III, adorned with ornate art nouveau lamps, gold-plated cherubs, nymphs, and winged horses dancing in the evening sky. This beautiful structure, like much of modern Paris, was built for the Universal Exhibition of 1900 and remains as majestic as ever.

As we sailed along, images evoking the final days of Royal France appeared before us, with Louis XVI and Marie Antoinette indulging in a decadent royal lifestyle. Life was meant to be savored, and we savored it fully that evening.

Our laughter echoed along the Seine, carried away by euphoria. By the time the boat reached a bend behind Notre Dame, fueled by fine spirits, our imagination transported us back to the Paris of centuries past, making it a truly royal affair.

It was undoubtedly a celebration arranged by our producer, Geoff, and those few hours were etched into our memories forever. Geoff remained my producer for life, proving his legendary status once again.

CHAPTER 11
The dark side of life.

I n a story filled with light, one mustn't overlook the darker side of adventure, especially while managing one's profession and embracing life to the fullest.

It had been raining incessantly that winter in London, so I yearned to escape to a land of tropical luxury, which may have seemed a bit extravagant, but I requested a transfer nonetheless. The agency, with eighty full-service offices worldwide, initially refused, but they knew I was serious and eventually offered me transfer options. I desired a year away, but they insisted on a three-year contract. Although I obtained the benefits of the transfer, such as a car with a chauffeur, a rent-free luxury home in the vibrant Yaba area, and a team of staff, they insisted on the three-year commitment.

They didn't reveal the exact location until I arrived, and to my surprise, it was Nigeria, now a democratic state in its fifth year of independence from Britain. The agency provided a twenty-five-page analysis of the hard facts about Nigeria, which I signed without thoroughly reading the fine print. They assured me that English was spoken, sort of, and emphasized the tropical climate with year-round sunshine, except for a brief rainy season in July and August.

Packed and ready, I embarked on a swift and luxurious British Airways VC10 flight, captained by the experienced and distinguished Captain Richard Boda, a former RAF officer.

Upon arrival at Lagos airport, a few Nigerian office staff greeted me, but the flight was unnerving as I accompanied a senior Barclays bank officer who seemed inebriated from gin consumption. He warned me that Nigeria was in the midst of a civil war and urged me to turn back immediately.

Nevertheless, we landed safely, thanks to the "juju" singers who believed their magic powers ensured safe landings for aircraft.

A red Opel driven by a truly inebriated driver transported me, along with some office staff, to a welcoming celebration at the Ikoyi hotel on an island in bustling Lagos. The leader of the event was my boss-to-be, "Olding," an old military man who seemed to be in the twilight of his life. Nonetheless, he was my boss, and I began an adventure that was both comfortable and strange.

During the evening at a joyous restaurant by the South Atlantic coast, a shocking scene unfolded. A heated argument between two men in tribal clothing escalated, representing the competing tribes of Hausa and Igbo. Suddenly, a tribal Hausa man shot the Igbo man seated at a table across from ours, resulting in a gruesome and blood-splattered tragedy. The horrifying sight left me sickened and frightened, yet I was told it was an everyday occurrence, part of the ongoing civil war.

To distract from the horror, my new friends invited me to wander the crowded streets of the market, where beggars sought relief. I had the protection of Robert, my 6'4" Hausa security guard, who reminded me that I was amidst a bloody civil war. Sadly, I hadn't read the report warning about the political upheaval before departing London.

In the midst of this disorienting experience, I encountered a child begging with her keeper. The child had only one eye in the middle of her forehead, just above her nose. Despite her condition, she radiated a captivating charm, and I couldn't help but feel drawn to her. Later, I found out she had a rare condition called cyclopia. Years later, I discovered that this remarkable little girl was living in Bermuda.

CHAPTER 12
A little background.

*Idowu A treasure who saved
my life three times.*

The birthplace of CocaCola, from the Kola nut (according to Nigerians).

A car is driven off the road, and another near disaster for the author

My time at the office revolved around confusion. Nigeria consisted of three major tribes: the Hausas (pronounced Howza) in the north, tall Islamic people who abstained from alcohol; the Igbos (pronounced Eeebos) in the south-east, and the Yorubas (pronounced Yoribu) in the south-west— both Christian. This newly independent democracy also encompassed numerous smaller tribes led by tribal chiefs struggling to survive. Their accents were challenging for a Canadian like me, resembling the sound of gargling water. They couldn't pronounce "Canadian," so they referred to me as a "Canna." Strangely, they seemed to dislike Americans but had some respect for their former rulers, the British, leading to their decision to accept a Canadian as a representative. In the years to come, I would write a book titled "Democracy Shot Dead," summarizing many intricate details for interested readers. It turned out to be Africa's first civil war, claiming over a million lives during the conflict, while I, a Canadian businessman, was merely sent to witness the explosion of turmoil.

As an advertising man or a loosely labeled Creative Director, my task was to find Nigerians or global clients who would hire me to sell their products to millions of Nigerians and help them survive. This proved to be an incredibly difficult challenge, given that many locals didn't fully comprehend the complicated English language.

A few days after my arrival, I arranged a staff gathering to have a chat. One question that arose was how I managed to get there. On the wall hung a map with a drawing of Europe and Africa on the left side, and North and South America on the right. I stood up and pointed to Toronto on the right side, where I departed from, demonstrating how I landed in London on the other side of the map before flying straight down to Nigeria. My explanation elicited a doubtful response from the audience, with one person asking if the world was split or how I managed to fly off one side and end up on the other by landing in London. It seemed incomprehensible. To lighten the mood, I served drinks and roasted corn.

Returning to the topic of our clients, one of them was a Rhodesian company seeking us to sell their products, like pills, to the vast Nigerian population, promoting full and healthy lives. I inquired about the content of these "magic" pills, and the manufacturer nonchalantly replied that they were mainly made of crushed bones, cleverly shaped into pills. He chuckled, stating that the people would never know.

Another client was selling Italian cars to

everyday Nigerians. The agency would gather a group of locals to sit on the ground while they projected a film of the car on the side of a white van. Some would drink a concoction made from Kola Nuts, which would later be sold worldwide as Coca Cola. In reality, the audience could hardly afford to buy a bicycle.

Rubber tires were sold after placing newspaper ads in local papers. We sent copies of these ads to our clients, European tire producers, embellishing them with false mastheads from "phoney newspaper ads" as evidence of their sales efforts. In reality, the papers didn't exist, and the European tire makers were duped out of millions.

Beer like Guinness was promoted with the magic line, "It'll give you power," suggesting that drinking it would enhance sexual prowess. It was another baseless campaign that continued for years, selling to a market that believed a big lie.

In this land, lies and distortion of facts thrived, where "Dash" was the key survival tactic to make big profits. "Dash" meant paying people off for things they claimed to have done or would do but never actually did.

But what was genuinely happening in this five-year-old democracy? At best, they were all starting to speak a common language, English, with 180,900 words in dictionaries that the locals struggled to understand. This posed a tremendous challenge for a struggling population accustomed to speaking hundreds of different tribal or regional languages.

CHAPTER 13
What was really happening?

There was a secret association operating in a bar known as the "Ikoyi Club" in Lagos. Although there were other discreet meeting places, I knew this one well because I had frequented it before in this once happy and thriving land. The bar in the "Ikoyi Club" attracted a strange, but inebriated crowd of expats from Britain, the USA, Germany, Holland, and even an ambassador from Czechoslovakia, among others. They were hatching plans and conspiring to ensure the downfall of this five-year-old democracy. One of them claimed to work for Nigeria Airways, but he never explained his role. I overheard their discussions, and it was chilling—they were plotting to kill thousands of leaders and influencers, from politicians to military figures and businessmen. Their sinister plans involved bombings and assassinations, intending to make these incidents look like accidents when reported in the newspapers. Their objective was to destabilize the government so they could exploit the immense wealth generated from selling "white oil" to international markets.

The rumors spread, and many pointed their fingers at an Anglo-Dutch company in particular, along with other junior partners involved in this bloody mess that was about to explode.

I attended these drunken brawls only twice, until they caught onto my views, and then I was out, becoming the target of as many as seven brutal attempts on my life. Strangely, I didn't take it seriously; I often laughed because, as a Canadian, the whole bloody thing seemed so ludicrous. Picture a dozen or so expats and one Nigerian newspaper journalist gathering, getting drunk, and making plans to destroy the very essence of maintaining a democracy. It certainly wasn't to guarantee the freedom of the people of Nigeria. It was so unbelievable that I saw them as drunken layabouts.

I couldn't fathom that these scruffs came from the civilized world, plotting to get their hands on the billions of dollars that big white oil would generate and divert it into the hands of selected individuals in the Nigerian political and military establishment. And if anyone got in their way, they would be eliminated. They even entertained the idea of forming a breakaway nation where big White Oil was first discovered in 1958. They called it white oil because they believed it belonged to the white races. I never took it seriously; it was almost comical. But it appears that it will happen in a region soon to become the breakaway state of Biafra, where oil was first unearthed for shipment overseas, leading to staggering profits.

CHAPTER 14
Death soon knocked at my door.

S oon, a million deaths struck like lightning.
There was blood on the streets, in the
laneways, in offices, and Akintola, the Premier
of Western Nigeria, was captured and dragged
through the streets until he was decapitated.
Thousands more were hunted down by gangs and
paid royally for their bloody deeds. These were
the men that Prime Minister Lester Pearson
had partied with a short while ago. The status
politicians and military leaders were other prime
targets, ready to be blown away. The leaders of the
assassination teams grabbed millions as the final
war on the land, in the sea, and in the air drew
to a conclusion.

Early on, I became a target, betrayed by a once
loyal Igbo manager in my office who reported
my every move to groups that tracked me down,
including at a joyous wedding where my car was
awash in flying bullets.

After the third attempt on my life, I approached
the Canadian Consulate in Lagos and asked for
help. It was sheer luck that the Canadian Prime
Minister, Lester Pearson, was in Lagos trying to
settle troubles in Rhodesia. In a panic state, I passed
a handwritten note to one of Pearson's guards while
they walked into a major meeting.

Then everything went quiet until a Canadian spy named "Turnip" was instructed to get me out of Nigeria discreetly without further attempts on my life or the lives of my associates. And she did.

To do this, I was breaking the law for sure, but it wasn't my decision, it was a decision made by "Turnip" as the only way Canada could get me out safely.

First, citizens of the country were instructed that foreign money was not to leave the country. In response, "Turnip" packed the inside of my boots with British pounds sterling. I was walking on thousands of pounds, and it was uncomfortable. Second, the devious plan had me leaving on a local Nigerian Airways DC6 headed to Kano in Northern Nigeria. Then, as a precaution, she insisted I get drunk on rum and coke as an excuse if I am captured.

But the final very dangerous move was a maneuver I had to make. When the domestic DC6 flight by Nigerian Airways to Kano was announced, I was to appear to be heading to board it. I waited until I was the last passenger boarding that flight, then I changed my direction and ran behind a barrier heading for an Alitalia flight in the international departure gate, boarding for Rome, which happened to be leaving at the exact same time.

I do not know how I made it, but it was all coordinated by a dozen Canadian spies scattered around the airport under the command of the infamous Turnip. It was pure magic as the alternative useful ticket to Rome was stuffed in my left stocking, along with other critical information, like a letter saying my father had died, and I had to rush home to Canada. The exit was silky smooth, and the paperwork was cleverly hidden in my other stocking. Anyone stopping me was to be paid in dash money passed to anyone trying to get me on the Kano flight with a flick of my wrist. It worked, and I was free and took off at 11.05 pm from Ikeja airport, a mere 5 minutes late. The surprise was the appearance of "Turnip," who was also onboard. Naturally, she smiled and ignored me.

Once in the air, I was sworn to secrecy and to never talk about "details" nor the people involved for fifty years. Despite the shattering blows of departure, I tried to tell my story, but was reminded by the Canadian diplomatic corps in Ottawa to keep it away from the media, and that was it.

Today, I still admire their diplomatic skills and cunning efforts, without harm to any Canadians. This story became somewhat public with the release of my book "Democracy Shot Dead ©," followed by film and TV offerings that may appear in the future. However, the full story with its harrowing details still remains a secret to this hour.

CHAPTER 15

It's a bird, it's a plane, and it's super incredible.

After my escape from the now rebuilt state of Nigeria, I was flown to London with stops in Rome, Paris, Vienna, Frankfurt, Berlin, and Rotterdam, "presumably" to heal from the damage. The escape was a gift from the silent Canadian government spy players.

Upon touching down in Toronto, I had another gift for my dear English-born wife, Beverley, from a mysterious and loving donor. It was one hell of a present, brilliantly clever and always to be remembered. It was a gift from members of my profession.

There was only one way to cross the Atlantic in

four and a half hours, have a magnificent dinner with exceptional views we would never see again, and then have dinner in London on the same day we departed Toronto, and hopefully, a chance for my dear wife to dine with her father.

What made it even more spectacular was that it was on December 24th. Crazy, yes. Ludicrous, oh yes. Forever memorable, of course.

It was a rare one-way trip on the unbelievable flying bullet, Concorde, the fastest means of travel in the world at the time, and all in dreamlike luxury. We shot like a bullet from Lester Pearson's runway, headed towards James Bay for a reason I will never understand, and then we turned and swung east, heading back from high in the blue sky, straight to London Heathrow airport in a brief 4.5 hours.

Only 100 passengers were on board, in twin seats on each side, in luxury fit for a king. A short walk down a wide aisle led us to be welcomed by Captain Richard Boda (who never left the cockpit). He was the same captain who practically crushed my hand with his hefty grip a while back. I reminded him that he was also the captain who piloted a BOAC VC10 flight to Nigeria in 1962. The wife and I laughed for the rest of the journey, with one exception. When the Concorde reached its maximum speed and broke the sound barrier, there was an announcement.

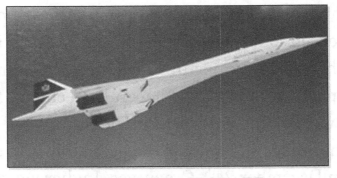

CONCORDE AIRCRAFT

I reached out and touched the window of the tiny airship, and it was surprisingly hot, with a captivating deep plush blue view through the small window and a shrinking sunset forming behind us.

But we didn't care. We were downing our second glass of champagne and cheering for the good life for the fortunate, who would be laughing forever. No, we'd never let the fun be forgotten as we'd been blessed yet again.

In that moment, in a dreamlike state, I was reminded of a song by the Alan Parsons Project that will not be forgotten.

The lyrics are something like, "Time flowing like a river, Time beckoning me - Who knows if we shall meet again, if ever - as Time keeps flowing like a river, to the sea, Goodbye my love, maybe forever, goodbye my love - Time waits for you. Who knows when we shall meet again, if ever, but time and good memories keep flowing like a river, on and on, to the sea."

CHAPTER 16
A wonderful ring in my ears.

Chasing the vibes

Celebrating a new head office

After returning to Toronto, another surprise awaits. A phone call from someone called David in New Zealand - who is David, I recall thinking? I don't know him, but he wants to meet in Toronto in two days for a luxurious lunch. It's an offer he is about to make, asking if I'll join his advertising agency in tiny New Zealand as the Creative Director. London has advised that I need a break, and this is the ideal place to relax and rebuild the family, both emotionally and physically.

Once again, London steps in with a lovely pat on the head and is the reason for the call, as it's the same agency group. Yes, I am thinking, the family needs a break and from what I know, this is the perfect place for a loving family with two daughters, Michelle and Nicole, and my wife Beverley.

On January 14th, we're in the air, but flying the

long and slow way. First to London to say goodbye to Beverley's Dad, then a hop to Dubai in the Middle East, a long leg to Hong Kong, then Tokyo where my golden-haired children were a hit, finally another long hop to Fiji, and finally through a tropical storm to bed in beautiful Auckland. Yes, it would have been half the time on Concorde.

We were met by my new friend David in Auckland and driven to our luxurious new home on Victoria Avenue in conservative Remuera. We'll be living in what is really a diplomat's home, as he is on assignment in Australia for a few years. Sheer beauty awaits in this tiny island that is like no other on earth. My daughters have been enrolled in private schools a few paces from our new home, and life will be a dream mission like nothing before. We walk and whistle, breathing in the intoxicating fresh air everywhere we go. I have a car, and a second car awaits my wife, a Mini, and she loves it.

What I will never forget is the aroma of fresh flowers everywhere we travel. And the Kiwis are such welcoming people, they made us feel like family that we'd known for a lifetime.

We were introduced to David's wife Anita and their little ones, Matthew & Amanda, and others like Therese, Beth, Michael, Andrea, Robin, Terry, Mike, Tim, Nicole, Kevin, Jane, Julie, and Blackie as the Radio Hauraki on-air gang, who became dear friends within minutes. The accent is as clear as a bell, with the exception of an inability to say the number 10. It always lands on my ears as "tin," but it is a source of international affection, not an irritant. And winter is simply a blink before the sun appears again in the southern hemisphere. No, I am not a travel agent, but I recommend everyone visit this enchanting island before they say they've lived life.

As for the professional creative pleasures, it can never, ever be beaten. My clients included everything from the South Pacific's finest cookie manufacturer, named Aulsbrookes, to the world's finest manufacturer of rugs and carpets, with the appropriate name Feltex. And everything in between, from Nivea cosmetics to crackers called Cruskets. My staff is unbeatable as well, including one of the finest art directors I've ever worked with, a Maori and certainly the first I'd ever call "the best." There is no need to replace anyone; they are all better than me.

In my tenure in New Zealand, the office began operating from stuffy quarters in Remuera to luxurious offices in a spectacular setting in downtown Auckland, built for us three years later. Every Friday, all of our clients would get together in the office rear garden for a social few hours while drinking and sharing laughs like never before. And laughter was the key event with all of the crowds.

The country is surrounded by the South Pacific's greenest seas, so we spent the bulk of our leisure days sailing around the beautiful harbor and out to the sea. In everyone else's sailboat, of course - hell, it beat working. Even the queen paid a visit, allowing all citizens to wave at her as she was driven around One Tree Hill in her royal limo, of course. The Royal New Zealand Navy band would provide the usual Royal pomp and circumstance, while the Prime Minister, dubbed Piggy, gave the customary screech from the balcony. This is life, living in beautiful New Zealand with a human population of almost five million, and a few million more, but they were sheep.

Business went through an incredible growth spurt over that time. And assignments kept me in the air, traveling between Australia and locations around the world on major productions. The Aussies were also a wonderful lot to work with - between the put-downs and the beer, there was more beer to enjoy. And the travel was flying Qantas or Air New Zealand first class, which was far more than anything I had experienced. But we all felt right at home and never wanted to leave. It is fair to say I was busy from the moment we set foot on Kiwi soil to our departure years later, along with the addition of three "kiwi cats" to frolic in Canada's snow three years later, named Victoria, April, and Chantilly, who would make life remarkably joyous for immigrant cats forever.

CHAPTER 17

Adventure awaits each South Pacific day.

One of our clients, Feltex, is the world's most prosperous maker of all-wool carpets, found everywhere from the UN in New York to Buckingham Palace and luxurious abodes around the globe.

The three big carpet designers, David Turner, Marion Newman, and Brian Todd, have a reputation as the best in the world. Unless you were a Kiwi, you wouldn't know they had such stars. But with their sheep and wool, they cleverly craft quality carpets. Another impressive fact is that they spend up to five months making one batch of various sizes of carpet.

This year, Feltex decided to introduce a new range of carpets called the "Feltex International Designer Collection," designed by their top trio. Marion Newman will design the splashy and colorful Vogue collection, while David Turner, who looks more like a farmer than a designer, will create the posh and conservative Landscape Collection. But this year, they decided to add Frenchman Pierre Cardin as a designer for their Pierre Cardin collection, to add a little extra zip, splash, and price.

Meanwhile, Brian Todd, who graduated from Kidderminster College (the Cambridge or Oxford of the carpet world), will design the Cairo Berber collection. Sensuality, they all agree, is important for a carpet. It has to feel good, so the first thing potential customers must do when selecting a carpet is to touch it.

We decided that television would be the primary media in both Australia and New Zealand, and sixty-second commercials were a must. However, the commercials had to be filmed with the designers speaking on location. Marion would be filmed in New York at the UN; Brian Todd in Cairo, and David in a post-English estate set in the beautiful English countryside.

The question was: how the hell could we do it, as we'd have to travel 46,436 kms around the world to achieve great results. The designers agreed it couldn't be done in the time allocated, and the cost would be prohibitive. They joked that they might look like babbling idiots with rural accents when the camera is switched on.

My role was to make it sound easy and make the experience a thrilling one for the designer stars, soon to be TV personalities in Australia and at home in New Zealand.

CHAPTER 18
We're off, and we'll have an enjoyable time, again.

B ut how can I tell them it'll be a laugh, when I'm the one who'll be hung by the fingers if the production falls flat on foreign shores? So, I must provide positive leadership and believe in the skills of the production staff who will have to travel with the team to keep watch. And what a whopper financially, but I believed Feltex was confident, because I asked them to feel that way. That's how it works.

So, we had three designers, a producer, a director, and myself – the Feltex team. Then we'd add local production crews in the three locations: New York City, Cairo, and London. Sounds doable, but we also have to take carpet samples/swatches with us, as they cannot be picked up at each filming location. No, it's beginning to feel impossible, maybe nuts, but I really did feel good, as all I had to do was watch the performance of the designers in front of the camera, unless they're bumbling idiots who cannot remember their lines. Then it'll work well, but management will say bye-bye, mister creative, if it doesn't work, and it'll cost Feltex a flipping fortune.

During the flight, the designers were caught attached to their scripts, trying to remember 60 seconds of pitch for the entire duration of the journey – with failure painted on their faces. It's no fun, just nervous tension, but the odd beer loosened their tongues and improved their magnetic minds.

When we arrived in New York, it was a snap. Great American crew, but they wanted cash up front. Off to the bank, the money was ready in no time. Everything worked, Marion was a first-class performer. We never got to the UN; they wouldn't allow us in, so we stayed in a nearby seedy hotel, set up a display with the carpet, while Marion spat out the script – take one, was in the can. A backup was recorded for insurance purposes, then we were off.

Next, we flew to London. The crew in the UK were miserable and gave us one location for filming, called The Manor House. If we didn't accept it, the filming would be brought to a halt unless we agree. Done, then we had an urgent call from Tim from the agency in Auckland, screaming, "DON'T FILM THE GREEN CARPET, it's been pulled from the lineup." Too late, we shout back, it's already been filmed. We'll have to get another carpet from somewhere – f—k the brand, anything grey will do. So another piece of carpet is hurriedly slammed on the floor and filmed quickly. They'll never know it's another maker, no one will ever know. We all agreed not to say a thing. Next, we're off to Cairo, but our timing is off, dammit.

Another problem erupts: Brian Todd has not been allowed to enter Egypt, nor the crew, so we must find another location that looks like the Middle East and get the carpet sample diverted to the new location. Oh double dam, they curse, but it's time to switch gears and solve the problem fast, as the Middle East portion filming Brian Todd, our cool designer, will be blown. Then we found a solution.

Done, we're off to Jerusalem, a new crew of Israelis will meet us at Ben Gurion airport in Tel Aviv. The producer boys in Israel are famed for solving impossible problems, like giving birth to a state, which was born in a state of chaos.

We landed with a bewildering welcome by the new Israeli team; they were sharp and a bit saucy and everything was mapped out. Brian Todd was remarkably calm, as we expected, or pissed. We motored down the Cross-Israel Highway to a location in Jerusalem, through barricades, then onward for an uncomfortable rest. But we made it to the set. It was ready to shoot with three Berber carpet samples on display in a market setting. Todd knew his lines and did the usual, first take presentation. The only problem was the goats who kept walking past the cameras and upsetting our props and abusing the extras we hired to walk through the location. It took thirty minutes because of the chaos, but hell, we wrapped the film segment with Brian.

One incident that startled me a bit was a crew member who generously gave me a cool snack. It was like a cone filled with something that resembled ice cream, but the ice cream looked like multi-coloured worms that appeared to be wriggling. No, they said, with a chuckle, they're not worms, so I gobble it down because it was a hot day and I needed to cool down.

It was so delicious; I whooped yet another sweet-lipper down. But the Israeli crew had a chuckle when they admitted it was indeed filled with little coloured worms and that most Israelis ate them as a treat on a hot day. Yuk, I hurried back to the plane to catch a flight home. I had to catch it via London Heathrow, but I was quite ill all the way back to dear London.

I've been researching what was in the cone for years, with no results to date. Most said it was a bit of a farce, sure I said. Time for a rest.

Then I landed back in Auckland after a long, long journey, this time it had me laughing most of the way.

CHAPTER 19

A diversion around the world that we'll all adore.

Before we returned to Canada, I did another crazy thing, I decided to take my daughters on a worldwide trip around the world from Auckland to Fiji, to Bombay, India where the plane was simply gassed up, for the next stage of the flight to Cannes, France to pick up an award I had won years earlier for Phonogram; it was a sixty second cinema commercial for a up and coming British band called Godley and Cream – titled "Consequences", then onward to England to meet with our British friends and Beverley's father; then onward to Toronto to be sure our Canadian home was still there, then off to Hawaii, for a brief sunshine holiday break then finally to Auckland. For a final rest and time to pack for our final, final, final trip back to Canada.

CHAPTER 20
This is finally it.

T he final journey from Auckland with the family was a peaceful one, filled with more laughter and plenty of grub. We started to do a final pack while having a few get-togethers with old friends. Athletic daughter Nicole, a super runner, was proudly wrapped in her Corran green gear from school, and Michelle, our resident violinist, was home after a walk from Victoria Avenue. We dashed off to dine with David Murphy and his family, followed by an outing at our favorite Georgie Pie restaurant to say goodbye to their delicious beef pies, chicken pies, and more pies, and of course, more old neighbors.

The three years were truly remarkable, and our blessed Kiwi buddies will remain beloved friends forever. Memories of living a unique and exceptional three years of absolute fun will never be forgotten. All topped off with the nicest and most decent people on the planet.

The event we really missed about Canada was the white Christmases, our extended families and relatives, and the sight of snowflakes falling. While in New Zealand, we were amused by the Kiwi version of Christmas because the tree was simply a big branch, and they depicted jolly old Santa sitting in a sleigh being pulled by a school of fish?

On the final day, we lifted off for Fiji to catch our Canadian Pacific first-class flight to Toronto. After a tear-filled goodbye to friends from Beverley and the children, Michelle and Nicole, our newborn water babies who loved to run and swim in the clear and beautiful aromatic airs of our South Pacific water lands, the departure will never be forgotten. Why should it be?

We arrived home in Toronto with our feline friends and a waterfall of memories that will indeed last beyond a lifetime. Thank you, dear Kiwi friends.

CHAPTER 21
At last, we're first.

The journey back home left no time to rest; it was the place where my inner businessman had to be at his best. Now, it's an opportunity to be inventive once again, back in the homeland at last. I had promised that the fun would continue just as before, but this time, it had to be a successful endeavor while embracing the challenges of life and striving for a normal existence. Our goals were clear: we needed to build savings quickly for retirement and ensure our children received a proper education, all while securing a comfortable life for ourselves when we retired.

The first obstacle emerged when we discovered that Canada had been quietly invaded by American conglomerates, who devoured the creative advertising and communications industry that I had spent a lifetime building. This shock came after a free trade deal was signed by Ronald Reagan and Canada's Brian Mulroney in 1988, allowing American giants to dismantle and assimilate Canadian-owned businesses.

However, I had a plan to open a communications company dedicated to our country, and I was determined to succeed once again. The old Canadian businesses had sold out to American shops, but Campaign House International was born, and we had clients like Panasonic, Goodyear, Bauer, and Canstar. We joined IMPA, an international marketing group, and while working with them, we proved that loyalty to our own countries and nurturing local clients and staff is the way to thrive.

Our motto was to "Outsmart the elephant (Americans) and feed the mouse steroids," and it became widely known and emulated by other nations. One memorable success was launching "The International Express" newspaper in Canada and then in the USA, which brought us into contact with outstanding writers and led to exciting parties with the Hollywood elite.

As our reputation for excellence spread, more business flooded in, and we even struck a similar deal with another big British paper, securing 50%

ownership of the venture. Eventually, the time came when I decided to retire and bid farewell to the business. Bates, a global agency, bought our company, and after some reselling, it ended up in the hands of Saatchi & Saatchi.

To conclude, I apologize to readers for any discrepancies in the timing of events or the spelling of names. I acknowledge that my memory might not be as sharp as it once was. Lastly, I extend an enormous thank you to CSIS, MI6, and the British based Christianson Deman Advertising group, without whom my journey wouldn't have been as filled with laughter and success.

THE AUTHOR

D. Richard Truman was born in the steel city of Hamilton, Ontario, Canada and began his writing career after a stop at Ryerson University, as an advertising copywriter in Toronto.

During his forty-five year career, he worked with major international advertising agencies in North America, Europe, Africa and Australasia, developing communications campaigns for Air Canada, General Motors, Phonogram, Chrysler Europe, Panasonic, Ford, Wrigley's, General Mills, Feltex, Burger King, The Government of Canada and many, many, scores of other worldwide brands.

After twenty-five years employed in the international market, he returned home to Canada. A few years later he set up his own company, Campaign House International, which emerged as the Canadian nucleus of a worldwide group of "boutique" agencies, a considerable achievement in a savagely competitive industry dominated by foreign, notably American and British mega-agencies

Nearing retirement, Truman sold Campaign House International to Bates, part of the Cordiant Group plc, of London, England.

SUMMARY

The 615.20 trillion dollar global advertising business titillates observers with ongoing controversy and don't-tell-all adventures starring heroes and swine in a profession, perceived to be laced with cut-throat skullduggery, but not. It is a highly skilled professional and necessary competitive force that informs us, to keep competition alive and prices competitive in every walk of life.

Advertising is a muscular force that loves us when we listen but shames us if we don't

This is Truman's 11th book. He currently lives in Burlington, Ontario with his wonderful wife Beverley, their two daughters, five grandchildren and a lovable cat called Ozzie, and a pesky mouse.

Printed in the United States
by Baker & Taylor Publisher Services